Broken Mirrors

Broken Mirrors

Yoon Sik Kim

The New York Quarterly Foundation, Inc.
New York, New York

NYQ Books™ is an imprint of The New York Quarterly Foundation, Inc.

The New York Quarterly Foundation, Inc.
P. O. Box 2015
Old Chelsea Station
New York, NY 10113

www.nyqbooks.org

Copyright © 2012 by Yoon Sik Kim

All rights reserved. No part of this book may be used or reproduced in any manner whatsoever without written permission of the author except in the case of brief quotations embodied in critical articles and reviews.

First Edition

Set in New Baskerville

Layout and Design by Raymond P. Hammond
Cover Photo by Yoon Sik Kim

Library of Congress Control Number: 2012949936

ISBN: 978-1-935520-69-6

Broken Mirrors

Acknowledgments

Originally, poems in this collection appeared in the following publications: *Green Mountains Review*, *Chants*, *Midland Review*, *Pleaides*, *Black Bough*, *Voices International*, *Rhino*, and mostly *The New York Quarterly*.

*for Ariel, Sarah, Kathryn, and Beverly,
Angels on Earth*

CONTENTS

EARLY MORNING BIRDS IN FLIGHT / *13*
AUTUMN / *15*
CONVERGENT EVOLUTION / *16*
DENUDEMENT / *18*
THE FOG OF WAR / *19*
IMAGINATION / *21*
BORN ON THE 4TH OF JULY / *22*
GWENLIN, CHINA / *23*
PLATOON / *26*
THE BEHAVIOR OF MIKE, THE CHIMP / *27*
THIN, OVERNIGHT FOG, ON THE PRAIRIE / *28*
L' IMPRESSION DE DEGAS / *29*
THE UTTERANCE / *30*
THE PEASANT J. BUVIER / *32*
CHURNOBULL IN 1990 / *33*
GRACE UNDER PRESSURE / *34*
THE DAWN / *36*
A DESERT POOL / *37*
THE DEATH OF VOYAGER / *39*
UNBENDING REEDS / *40*
I, THE INTERPRETER / *41*
COLD FUSION / *43*
A LETTER OF RECOMMENDATION / *45*

A CEILING FAN WITH A BULB / 47

LIVING WITHIN / 48

A HERO WITH A THOUSAND FACES / 49

L'ENFANT TERRIBLE / 51

TORNADO: WIND THAT WINS / 53

PRIMA DONNA COYOTE / 55

ODE TO WINTER / 57

PRESSING THE AIR / 59

HERE STANDS THE AGED HAMMURABI, ALL FLESH AND BLOOD / 61

HAIKU / 63

AT A LOCAL WATERMELON SALE / 64

A STOP AT THE BLACK HILLS / 65

RIVER COLORADO / 69

NOCTURNE / 70

MEDITATION / 72

AT THE HEART OF SAHARA / 73

GHOST PAIN (FROM AN AMPUTATED MEMBRANE) / 74

DEAD BROOK / 76

SPRING AT BOSNIA / 77

EMPTY / 79

UNDER THE AUTUMNAL SILVER MOON / 80

A TORRENTIAL RAIN / 82

A KID-PREACH IN THE PLAYGROUND / *83*

CONDORS / *84*

AN ARTIST / *85*

HERE LIES THE LAST BREED THE CHEETAH / *86*

CAR AIR CONDITIONER / *88*

THE DEALER / *89*

LOOKING AT THE MAP OF AFRICA IN BLACK, WHITE, AND GRAY / *90*

A POET / *91*

A BLIND DATE / *92*

AT THE CENTER / *94*

THE SORROW OF THOREAU / *95*

IMPLOSION / *97*

COGITO, ERGO SUM / *99*

JULY FULL MOON / *101*

DAO OF LAO-TSE / *102*

Broken Mirrors

EARLY MORNING BIRDS IN FLIGHT

grand children of dinosaurs
in small groups vociferous

leap into the time
from invisible branches

defying the gravity the chain the air
they adrift in geological time

in blue waves

the leaves of memory hide
their boisterous claims

and now long dead the tree too
deprives them of their original rights

the landing sites
they must return to somehow

to brood

archaeopteryx feathers
the frozen flesh of the bird

captured in the fish-scale jaw
of the limestone rock

caught in the act
of evolution

the jump

arrested by the skeleton-thin barbed wire
the red-rusted iron frame

gestures flying wings
a burning flame

that leaves
no clues

nor ashes

AUTUMN

Raspy locusts jar the thinning autumnal air.
The blue firmament shatters, bits of glass. My
soul is a mummy, the anguish drained. My guts
are dry—withered leaves—the blood clotted.

Someone, I smell, burns dust somewhere. Nightly
crickets' ballads shard my bedroom window,
a splinter in the large open eye. Void of light.
Insect stridulation fiddles on my eggshell nerve.
Transparent-blue veins under the artificial light.
It's autumn. I walk tall, a toothpick skeleton.

CONVERGENT EVOLUTION

miles and miles away
millions of wildebeests eat off the skin of
the volcanic ashes millennia old
still aging in the teeth of photosynthesis

swarms of black lice biting off
the green skin of the earth
and the volcanic ashes hide into
the thick tough hides of the beast

in the seasonal swell of churning waves
an earthly accident of paradise hangs
never on the past nor broods on the future
but on the now of the invincible wet blades

of green reality
the nibbling Thomson's gazelles pronking high
like brown fleas on the beast
as the thin thread of white dry dust-devil

barefoot walks across the brown landscape
twist-dancing its feminine gossamer tail
the ghost dance that foretells the coming dryspell
the regular visitor of death screening

the old and the dying and the unfit now
the volcano is dead with its mouth wide open
and the firebirds, not the lying phoenix,
converge in the open mouth of the volcano

flamingo-waltzing in the mood of Johann Sebastian
on the bitter salt lake where no other form can
dance to the tune of now to the melody of here
intoxicated by the soup du jour of fungi

these firebirds invite Egyptian eagles raising
their young on these red-jacket flamingoes
that dance in the mirage of afternoon heat visible
invisible swallowed by the tongue of arid wind

DENUDEMENT

snakes
unclad
their skin
every year
disrobing
the thinning
past for the
thickening now
that unfolds
in the muscle
of mind against
the harsher
elements and odds
we call living
one that we too
must let go
eventually
because we love
the constant
censorious
presence the pang
of forgiving and
not forgetting
the ring scars
in our memory
in silent tears
it registers
what our growing
brought in this
year's drought
into the gut-
essence of
our stem
axed by
a sudden
act of
will that
splits

THE FOG OF WAR

in the shades of the night
palm trees play a practical joke concealing
squadrons of black bats hanging upside
down in the caves of igloos

iron jaws of armors
insignificant like a toy
abandoned by a Bedouin child
breathe the serene balmy desert air

dressed to kill for the night
they take off one by one
hiding their hideous intentions
under the wicked radar-thin black-gossamer nightgown

you only hear their lean moaning as they come
just before they touch off fireballs
the pent-up anger that tumbleweeds across
the lone desert fields

no one knows for sure where the fireball landed
aided by the high-tech scalpel they often hit decoys
the silhouettes of fighter jets in the moonlight
those cubistic renditions of war gears on cement

in two dimensions their shadows dazzle the concrete
runway beyond the grasp of Image Intensifier
the night goggle every tadpole in the pond wears
to grab the tail of the living shadow

in the dark nobody knows the real figures
the damage the silhouette enemy aircraft endures
they fly above the wavelength beyond our touch
basking under and

above the ultraviolet electromagnetic spectrum
the rainbow of our perception
the truth of natural deception
that wars in the mind of the living dead

the desert sand leaves no signatures
the dunes dance beneath the wavelength of our reach
invisible like the copperhead sand viper
that hides the truth among the grains of doubts

IMAGINATION

Envision the lamp burning in the infinitude of
A dark Indian cave Gigantic
Temple
Haunted by rock craven Hindu images
Of Evils, tortured lights, and fat bats hunger-
Struck
—only to awaken the Universe Colossal
beneath the skin of Shiva
Aching.

BORN ON THE 4TH OF JULY

We are sorry that we took your job
We are sorry we moved into your house
We are sorry I am driving your Porsche
We are sorry I am riding on your waterbed
We are sorry your wife has an aching body
that ebbs and flows like a lunatic tide
We are sorry she had to abort your mission
We are sorry she had to adopt my mission
We are sorry you had to die syphiloid
We are sorry you maimed your main vein
We are sorry you became a vegetable god
We are sorry that your God became insane
We are sorry you suffer moral conflicts
psychological regressions and withdrawals
We are sorry you became so sophisticated now
We are sorry you are alive somewhere today
We are sorry you are sorry we are sorry
We are sorry you were born under
the spell of firecrackers under
the steam of warm beers and hot spirits
under the fume of fire-star-crossed skirts
under the hands of ill-prepared midwives
We are sorry for the day of Julie

GWENLIN, CHINA

In the beginning was
no Red China.
But a blue oceanic body of water
full of microcosmic marine Republicans,
the minute bricklayers of budding limestone,
the tiny building blokes of Confucius ferns,
that breathed the blue brine soda water,
feeding on carbon dioxide and green flesh of sunburst,
squeezing the bubbles of oxygen out
from the avalanche of H_2O molecules, discomposed,
in the gigantic factory machine work
of primogenital solution.

For eons,
the single-minded drive to conquer the sea
kept them alive in the stillness of making
under the tons of back-breaking water, churning.
Day and night, they chewed and spat their guts
into the atoms of sands, bits of glasses, snowing,
flowering, upon the unquaking sea bottom graveyard undead,
solidifying, layer after layer, the principle of *Tao*,
the melody and the bone of the universal harmony,
as inches of bricks gain the grain every year,
as the termite mounds bulge pregnant
with the hardened will, and stillness
scraped the blue ceilings
of the ocean continent China.

Eventually,
the brick layers' labor was paid off
and emptied the seabed,
and mummified boisterous neighbors

into the flowers of fossils of waves.
And their millennia-old limestone kingdoms pushed the skies
further out into the swart space
as the blazing primordial rays
baked their gut-petrified castles
that refused to crack for ages.
But the rigid regularity of torrential throbbing
pulsed in and hollowed out their essence
—the bamboo of Taoism—
that now flutes winds through
and through its self-absent melody.

Now, the sunrays cut deep
into the chasms of towering walls of limestone landscape
and the bottomless valleys drown echoes
that swallow its shadows broken.
Now, the daylight burrows its teeth
marrow-deep into the abysmal shades of heaven
as ancient and as venerable as those villages
that suckle on the riverbed
where the lime brews
through its cavernous
pores, the essence
of pure spring
sweet
water
that chuckles
through
the belly button
of a monk.

The deep-sunken forest of limestone still
disquiets the jagged silence that pierces puppy-white clouds
floating above the dark blue.
The titanic silence crowds in,
embosoms, and embalms the soul that beholds.
And one dreams of a white butterfly
that flies in and out
of the transcendental nirvana,
the divine unconsciousness,
the prelapsarian rhapsody
in sheer watercolors.

PLATOON

On a muddy screen somewhere
the big guys chase after the little ones
—domesticated dogs' inertia after wild geese.
In hot pursuit dogs even eat dogs and
shocked geese fly shooting droppings off at the dogs.

In the dry patch of the mud the little ones grow rice in
between the lulls of volcanic lava flow:
Nam piglets thrive on a can of worms from Sam,
particles of a hand grenade down the jungle under.

In the mud somewhere big guys rape little wombs
—a mere loss of territoriality (of a foxhole).
Because the sun is too hot, the day is too tedious, and
too chancy to practice touchdown with a cannon ball.

The jungle always deepens dark.
Thousands of disoriented deer hunters are unleashed
—to free the deer. Rice paddies are full of heavy rice crop.
The aromatic napalm blossoms asunder in the game park,
the fanfare for the common man!

In the end, even the big guys are tired:
they have become allergic to such a stinking foreign soil
and pack.
Now on, they say, "we must find a new meaning of life"
—the lotus of the mud—after all.

The unharvested rice in the muddy-dry pad is all half-burnt:
fried and pop-corned. And the movie is over.
So, let there be light!

THE BEHAVIOR OF MIKE, THE CHIMP

He was the lowest-ranking male in the group:
an absolute bottom dweller with no hope, he was
the number 11th male, *very* wet behind the ears.

Being a Joe-six-pack, everybody peckered him: he
had to subsist in the shadow of backwater, rummaging
through what the God species had littered

around this holy site, of wastebin, in the thick
of African jungle. The God-fearing chimpanzees
in the black night of mind called it Mt. Olympus.

One day Mike stumbled across a large empty tin,
a paraphernalia/icon of civilization Athena dumped
around the campsite in the thick of African jungle.

When he toed the hollow tin can, it rolled down
the dumpsite, clanging its empty mouth like thunder.
That day Mike discovered God hidden in the tin.

Its terrifying racket was not an ordinary tin din:
the pandemonium blast squeezed the hearts of
all the terror-drunken chimps into a size of a bean.

A can now rules over the souls in the night of mind.
The chimp drives around the best car, fornicates with
the choicest wenches—whenever, wherever, however.

The funny thing is his domain is quiet, very very quiet:
nobody has tried to undo his rumpus ruckus dustup.
In the night of mind, Mike would always thunderclap.

Mike has thus mastered the art of Zeus, the supreme.
Now when he smells a sense of insecurity creeping in,
he uproars his domain with a brouhaha hullabaloo.

THIN, OVERNIGHT FOG, ON THE PRAIRIE

Diaphanous, bare, breath of Diana
garter-belts, low, just above
the green pasture

Wet by her silken strip of nightgown
skirting the grass

A yarn of satiny wrap
collapsed upon
itself

Upon a cool pool of water,
standing still,
her perfume

lingers, nakedly,
touching the face
of reflection

of the night
dream

L' IMPRESSION DE DEGAS

to let your son be
an artist
one must prick him to death
and make him
be a lawyer

through the lies of eyes
a judicious mind sees
the necessity
of colors

the oxymoron of being

a ballerina on tiptoe
the silken Japanese umbrella
upon a toothpick
stands the center

of equilibrium
the needle of balance
a constant pricking toward
the epicenter of making

drawing the ugly woman bathing
in unforgivably awkward positions
the wild cat's instinct of pruning
the necessity of physical
conditioning

true to itself
an artist is one
who never arrives

THE UTTERANCE

every now and then
from the extremity of my nerve
this flake of voice
edges me

gasping for air like a maniac
a single strand of noise
rockets up
among the seaweed of thoughts

this delightful disturbance
this blade of biting burn
this phantom of sound
rips me across, and the tranquility
of my recurring existence shatters

in the thick of my meditation
this worm of thought
crawls out of my body and
I anguish all night wondering
what it was that I heard

this whisper of a distant thunder
galvanizes my disquieting nerve
and thoughts flash as the lightning
agony brings no tears

I must catch the breath of this whisper
that peels away like satiny silky snake
the body wear of a woman that I remember
with long smooth shapely legs

again and again
I hear this voice surfacing
unsurfacing
from the deep down
and I cleanse my temple
with the incense of burning cedar

THE PEASANT J. BUVIER

With a companion of a dog, his ghost haunted around a shack,
a leaf afloat amidst of miles of high sea of desert.
No one knew if he had lived there at all. The land was
known inhospitable and unyielding and bone-dry.

Under the dimmering candle, his wrinkled hands examine
thousands of acorns one by one by one long...into

the night of the desolate place. The wind scratches
the silence that swallows the habit of speech
under the sand, orchestrating the Moonlight Sonata.

His seasoned eyes unveil the acorn of life, the blue
print of the universe. His iron rod drives each of his
will-moistened seed into the sand hole. One seed just
as gingerly as the other. Only a few survives out of a
thousand. Every year for twenty years, his ghost, all
alone, in deafening silence, dances the same motion.

Thirty years later the desert overflows with fountains
of acorn sprouts. Now each oak tree, like a growing child,
speaks the universal language of life. The sand understands
them, the birds sing them, the animals listen, and man
learns. Upon the desert sand, a peasant wrote a poem.

His iron will melted the sand into drops of water
that blossom into oak trees, birds, animals, and man.
People thought it was a work of nature and designated
the desert a national park.

Whenever I step into a forest,
I should like to take off my shoes. I would like to listen
to the lines a peasant wrote in the shoveling silence
under the flooding light of desert moon. For fifty years.

CHURNOBULL IN 1990

The hoary ray of ghosts haunts this Cosmopolitan Museum
of Modern Art, a grave of time that enshrines the artifacts
uncovered from the reactionary era of a primitive mankind:
its undressed untouchables, arranged as they were alive,
inanimate the goose-down feathers in the deep blue—
a still-life caged in by miles within a frame of barbed wires.

Now, only the ghost of wind walks across the main street
impersonating the Sahara Act I, Scene ii, "Desertion."
The wind keeps the burning wintry air sane and preserves
this Hollywood Stage of Nuke Puke for the moviegoers.

The governmental music strangles the air 24 hours a day
and soothes the aching teeth of decaying particles.
The buildings, impressed by the choice of the funeral piece,
observe the official days of silence in lean shadows.

The macabre melody sinks gravely into the tomb of time
and the core still breathes the venom of revenge invisible.
And the childrens' ghosts sway the empty swing to the
desert music as they perform a Russian ballet on a tiptoe.

In the tomb of unsettling dust, time ages in thin layers.
And a largely surreal white stork builds a huge nest on top
of an abandoned chimney that breathes air. In silent labor,
the bird renders a 19th century painting: it Picassos the
gestures of a federal synthetic Cubist, of the Party.

GRACE UNDER PRESSURE

To prove this nonsense you travel
halfway around the world, dragging
your skirts and whisky bottles. Of course,

you make wind-holes into innocent lions,
water buffaloes, or gazelles—for what?
A snap shot with your gun bearers?

Or flock to Florida to avoid winters,
where, with your beer buddies, you strike
deep-sea fishing for a mad marlinespike?

At night, in tropical heat and martini, you
engage in the usual bar-hopping and bar-
brawls, boxing off with black untouchables.

You sure always knock out someone older
and weaker than you. Therefore, poorer
and unfortunate than you are. For what?

To prove this grace under poop? This tall
order for a short man like you? A tiny wee
wee aided by the big thunder-stick?

Life for you is but a strife, a fit to prove what
is loudly absent within—the bangs you hear
while you carry on your rickety ambulance.

A stagger, a show-off in Hollywood style. A puff
of cigar in the African jungle with gun-bearers,
cooks, books, and a *memsahib* bed-comforter.

You may have conquered fishhooks, frying pans, and grasshoppers. You may have flattened and tightened box springs, nuts, bolts, and screws.

Anybody with your kind of money, time, and talent could have done all these and more. But at what cost did you gain your grace, white boy?

THE DAWN

A batch
of new hatch-
lings scramble across
the asphalt-black runway
where the sinews of Poseidon breathe.

Burning the silent afterburner
of life, one sortie after another takes off
into the realm of eternity where turquoise water
churns cosmic orchestra.

The sand stirs brine waves
and black stars scuttle into
the blue night of the Atlantic.

And the fire ball on the horizon
turtles across the swart ocean of milky galaxy
into periplum.

A DESERT POOL

a flake of lake crowned
atop afloats above the cloud

on top of miles of long steep cliff rocks
columns of primordial stones standing mute
in Doric order enshrine the heaven and
support the roof of clouds
in the thick castle of
Grand Canyon

a tadpole of civilization
a palm of accident
wombs under the thin
skin of the rock

a Pleistocene
hibernation

once in a lifetime however
in an age of petrifying dry spell cometh
the wildebeests of raindrop
stampeding across barefoot
wounding the skin awakening
the dormant desire under
the thin sheet of the lake bed

the stampeding army boots of wildebeests
carpet bomb the desert floor and the dynamite teeth
of flowers conquer the moment

the mirage of miracle the spectacle of life
the moment of is

in the flake of lake tadpoles shrimps and snails
all hectic and busy waste their fleeting existence

preoccupied with the preparation
for the life to come

the beast of truth that comes and goes
once in a millennium
meanwhile the jagged teeth of desert wind
carve out the intestines of rocks
the sun licks the lake bed thin everyday
it unskins each layer alive

as primitive paintings of dinosaurs
on the vertical walls vertigo
the passing

THE DEATH OF VOYAGER

From the deep dark, from the heart of
deep space, cometh an electric screech,
a scratch hundreds of light-years away.

Consuming itself away on a cancer cell,
a candle of message flickers before our
eyes trying to monkey with its meaning:

A thin thread of cricket chirp drowned
in the bellow of plasma, the angry fire
solar wind hurricaning through vacuum.

Finally unwound, this old Swiss watch,
now a molten piece of lead, squeezes out
its last bubble of breath in God's closet.

UNBENDING REEDS

Wee

these unnatural natural weeds

eat guts alive,

unlike the unfamiliar familiar

ready-mades

that do not own

a spine.

Supple dancers, they bend readily even in easy breeze,

the wind that wounds not

their spines.

Nor do they pine away their misery

under water;

their spirit yet

unbroken

their souls crawl in the Lethe

in search of lightening

that drift in and out

of their shadows.

Their fingers measure

the sky.

I, THE INTERPRETER

I, the official mockingbird of the desert Iraq
the living mouthpiece of the once-dead Homer
I wreck in dark suite with British accent
reciting sonorous songs day in day out
to resuscitate the ashes of the desert bird

the living shield of words of Allah my mouth is
full of loose feathers, sand shifting every minute
by the propaganda whims—winds of commercial war
my tongue bites children and women like a sand viper
that swims across the ocean of sand, alone

dancing to the crooked tunes of dunes
I, the official mouthpiece of a wind instrument
the magpie with a bagpipe that bewitches the world
with mirages of tanks, the black beetles that swarm
the oil fields to feed and mate caught by the moment

that weighs heavy on the burdened shoulders of have-nots
I, the official grandchild of Homer, ancient cousin of
Hussein, brother to Hitler and disciple of Khomeini
I, the instrument that plays the words to dance to the
tunes of dunes, shifting by the living sand grains

that lack rain and brain in an arbitrary terrain
I, the official mouthpiece of the desert bird
that feeds on blood of brothers and lethal oxygen
that pulls your eyeballs alive in the heat of desert
I call upon tanks and troops of young blood foreign

to build up mirages of oasis, castles of sand from all
over the world to have another ritual of Charlemagne kind
I, the official singer of *Iliad* and *La Chanson de Roland*
I, the official mouthpiece of Allah, I, the wind instrument for world peace, I, the Homer of modern era.

I, the Focus Retina, I, the amber eyeball of scorpion rolling the Giant Green ball, I, the interpreter of the unreal, I, the seer of the real estate, I, the mouth full of loose sand, I, the magpie with a bagpipe, I, the toothpick of Homer, I, the assassin of Rushdie, I, I,

COLD FUSION

Will it happen in this life?
A man is pushing his forties.
A woman, her late thirties.

Two particles circling each other
around and around every morning.

No sound of colliding. Except the air.
The tunnel dug in their mind stretches
as far as six miles. Around the golf course.

Nothing ever gets accelerated here between the two
ordinary water molecules swimming in brine water.
Drops of tears urinating through their eyelids.

The golf course is wet-green,
a fusion that matters/antimatters.

Light years apart, two particles orbit under
the cool morning breeze that splits nothing.

Every morning he jogs six miles. She five.
The lean lane is carved between narrow
heartbeats among the trodden grass.

He has never been married.
She only once. A short quick combustion.

He does not know her.
Except for this flare of morning affair.

This business of pressing heavy breaths
against their will. This silly attempt to elongate
life an inch.

She feels the cool of the morning:
it drips through her sighs.

Will it happen in this life? Could she ever
step into his lane one morning and collide?
Turning themselves into a sudden supernova
that matters and antimatters?

A LETTER OF RECOMMENDATION

I have known this fellow very well:
he once visited my house a while back
and I had played tennis with him once.

Took a couple of my courses, too. Mostly
graduate hours about Shakespeare, Milton, and
Elizabethan Literature. Was a good student.

English is not his native tongue; however,
he speaks fluently and writes superbly.
This is one foreigner without any accent.

I gather he has a mastery of five languages:
English, Korean, French, Spanish, and German.
Also an alleged brief affair with a China girl.

In fact, he sounds as good as one of us:
I gather he had fooled a few native girls
over the phone but seldom to his bed.

An ex–Air Force Commissioned Officer in ROKAF,
he struck me as a rare international gentleman.
He observes his sworn codes of officer's conduct.

His participation in classroom discussion was very
active, always piercing, but never too intrusive.
(I have already stated his gentlemanly breed.)

I also gather he is a writer, a budding poet.
Have seen his poems and records of publications,
and I must admit his works are really impressive.

In fact, considering his young age, he *is* good.
He owns this lightning sense of perceiving
resemblance among heterogeneous elements.

He grasps complicated and complex situations
in a single blow of perception and can yoke them
by violence together. Kind like the Metaphysics.

But he is not a scholarly type. Researches will
bore him. He is not cut out for a traditionalist.
Rather, he fits better as a leader somewhere.

Possibly as an administrator, department head, or
even a dean, if not the president of a university.
His term papers were good, but less than superior.

A CEILING FAN WITH A BULB

Giant mandibles of a beheaded dragonfly,
of metallic luster, hang, pinned on the ceiling.
Its pair of wings purr, nailed alive, in electric
shock of whir, an instinctual motor on a de-
capitated brain, its bulging bug eyes long
dead.

LIVING WITHIN

Now that I am free and finally
out of cage, out of the career of being
a professional student, Bill says,
I should try and live within
myself.

I suppose he is right.
I have been living without. Too long.
No shadow walks upon my empty house.
And the passing wind is full of whims.
It leaves nothing but disturbed dust.

For a decade now I have lost my sole
in a foreign soil. My sight myopic.
An existence on the edge in the whirlwinds.
No vortex in vertigo.
Now that I am old enough, he says,
I must empty what I learned.
This beanbag full of garbage
a small sausage of knowledge well wrapped
in an aluminum-gilded gift package.

I must return to my empty house, he says
and deport these foreign ghosts full of wind.
I must undo what they did and I must, he says,
unlearn what they taught. This dust and all.
Aged and thick and undisturbed.

Find the voice of your own ghost, he says,
the ghost in exile deep inside
you once again be the master of your being
and once and for all storm free within
yourself.

A HERO WITH A THOUSAND FACES

He was just another perch in the local pond,
any of various freshwater fishes of the genus
Perca, an ordinary soul in a nameless world.

One day a local fisherman came to the pond,
hooked him in the jaw, a worm still hanging.
He was furious, for he was on fire with life.

He kicked, wailed, and hollered as much as
a perch could, sensing an imminent death:
burning in the hell of sizzling vegetable oil.

But the angler did not eat him: he wanted to
use the vibrant perch as bass bait, the large-
mouthed Death, ubiquitous in every water.

His small frame was just about the right size:
the angler threw away anything too big or
too small, and he happened to be lucked out.

As the angler baited him sharp on the back,
piss ran down through his knees from pain
and for the fear of the underworld journey.

At the bottom of the murky water, he met
the grim face of Death. Raw, it swallowed
him whole—this largemouth monster Death.

Then the angler snagged the black mouth, and
the Death himself was fighting for his dear life.
It was a hair-raising turn for the little perch.

Out of the open jaw of the Big Death, flew out
the perch, unscathed, somehow gotten off the
hook—his bean-size heart frozen in the ordeal.

He then shot into the vastness of the water,
his back still bleeding the dark fear of Death.
He was the smallest big fish that ever got away.

L'ENFANT TERRIBLE

Up in Rose Township, Michigan
a 3-year-old girl was found belatedly
on December 29, Circa 1993.

Amanda Iltis was barefoot:
no shoes, no socks, no gloves
clad scantily in a thin cloth coat.

There was no goat in the manger,
a '79 Chevy her mother crash-landed
when Mary's car ran off the road,

Hit a tree, popped the windshield,
killed Mary almost instantly, and
then came to rest in dense brush.

Mary was 29 years old, she was
on her way to a relative's birthday
party, and she was no virgin.

Three wise men came out of nowhere:
one in disguise of a passing motorist,
the other two as state troopers.

Amanda apparently crawled out
from her seat belt and huddled on top
of her mother's body, now losing fire.

The overnight chill dropped subzero,
and exposed the child to extremes.
Stars shone bright in remote skies.

15 hours later when the deputy touched
the little body huddled next to her mother,
the infant woke up, "My Mommy's dead."

Amanda suffered only bruises, a fracture, and minor frostbite. Later she recalled her Mommy's last words: "I love you."

TORNADO: WIND THAT WINS

Every Spring in Oklahoma comes a sudden
Baptist preacher that practices in tongues
of the ancient Greek Homer.

Unlike Billy Graham, his brother, he carries
his own Gargantuan tent, swart as soot thick
as his brassy lung.

His Hectoring grunt jumps every little bell
out of their sins and makes cows on the couch leap
on the run for a nearby ditch.

No creature stands against this preacher.
He owns a mouth as wide as a football field, and
his thundering rhetoric reaches as far as Kansas.

Right out of the blue, he crashes down quick
to shock and kick these plainsfolks' butts
into the tent of Southern Baptist Convention.

Just about this time of the year comes a sudden
Baptist preacher that pipes gospels in one
hundred miles per hour gust. He is disgusted.

He abhors branches of different denominations,
trashes ideas on the street, and he can't stand
the sinful matchboxes of mobile homes.

So Heaven must send its official mouthpiece.
A salesclerk that hoovers everything in God's way,
sucking brains out from each household.

Circa 1990, I too received his sudden visit.
And one visit was enough. That year I lost my
secretary, a porcupine-blonde concubine.

That year I lost my wife to the preacher, who
grabbed my mobile homes, too. That year I was

found by my three-year-old crushed under his blow.
That year I found Jesus.

PRIMA DONNA COYOTE

I quit the stage at the age of forty.
And ended my career of acting, playing roles
for the stage, for somebody, all together.
I was the third-time prima donna at that time,
a reddened plum at its prime among the troupe.

I was a born dancer with flexibility;
my motion brought grace among the brute.
The setting was perfect for performing:
my father was a preacher in Oklahoma
and I was his beloved only daughter.

My father choreographed the dance routine
precisely according to the written Script.
I was the ballerina of his choice, and
at eleven the world became my stage. My destiny
unfolded itself even before I asked:

I sang his songs, gestured his movements,
and saved many a stranded cattle into the tent.
I danced with him until one day John came to the scene.
At eighteen. We danced together ever since.
And everybody admired the perfect fit.

Now my body moved his movements, my mouth sang
his songs, my words spoke his, and I did his deed.
I was a born dancer full of grace, remember.
And we were inseparable as a shadow, stuck hard,
under the midday Summer sun in Oklahoma.

Then came along onto the stage my four children;
they, too, danced along with us as we thought fit.
I became their song and their voices. I became their
ferny fingers, feeling the world around, learning.
And learning did take its toll:

John grew a shadow in his chest. He thought that
I lingered a different heart in the closet. That my
voice unvoiced his, my movement no longer did mirror.
Ever since I returned to college, we grew aware of the
crack in the pot, a hole that sips the outside air through.

He trailed my tail wherever I went. He hounded me in my
dreams with a chain saw. But I still loved him dearly.
I could not let go of him. I thought of my children,
my father, too. For thirty-some-odd years. The dance
became painful, and to act was a cruel joke.

At forty-one, I now realized I was a born dancer.
Now I write my own script, choreograph my own movements,
and I even let him have his children. Alone, I dance
my own dance. Alone, I do not mind crying a bit.
All alone, I am finding myself, finally.

ODE TO WINTER

The green lion is finally,
dead. Defunct flat, de-
composed in brown.

And, yes, the winter firestorm
smokes on once again…

Icy blaze torches and tortures what
little remains out there.

Another wintry funeral pyre
in naked moonscape.

Frigid flames in.ci.ner.ate.
charred bones of fingers.
Cremated treetops are on fire.

Gray skies bubble smoke screen:
the sun dimes dim in the soot.

Ashen snowflakes drop and flop
like broken butterfly wings.

Fireflies of cinders, they are
returning souls.
Of the extinguished.

Hidden deep in the pile
of charred bones, for now

frozen like teeth,
hibernates the marrow.

The green dragon seed.

There it daydreams the Phoenix
and its golden wings.

There in the ashes, the egg
is asleep, lost in raging ire.
For now.

PRESSING THE AIR

My embrace is a beautiful embarrassment
a gasp of air, a bag of gesture

I espouse then collapse within
upon my shadowy
tight lead-dead weight

Every day I hug this bagful of vacant air
this *forma* that slips out of sight
in no time from my arms OUT
onto the realm of total
otherness

These are not my limbs
nor my lips

My sign is a caution of pantomime
a motion of the ocean
that ebbs and flows
the open emptiness

In the clanging wind
of an empty parking lot
where ghosts of souls
linger in a slow dance
like spent soda cans

I stretch my arms far out all day to fish the wind
to caress this intangible substantiality
I crave to feel the wind that breaks my bone-
less sleeves in half

I spread my broken white wings in the mimetic
gesture of Japanese cranes who pantomime

a ghostly dance unsynchronized
in the full dust of moonlight

Where a lone phantom steps upon its
own shadow and lingers
around the clock
attending the
air

HERE STANDS THE AGED HAMMURABI, ALL FLESH AND BLOOD

Again yesterday
a wild pack of Lebanese dogs
wearing the thin cloth of night
paid a weekend visit
to their beloved neighbor

        a squadron of Israeli soldiers
        sleeping in makeshift tents
        yet another barracks on a Newfoundland
        where generations of the indigenous had been
        digging up the soil with dirty fingernails

the unkind visitors with the night face
in no-nonsense black silk stockings
did not even breathe as they pitchfork
hays of soldiers by the throat
in the silence of love—in the making

        today at ten a.m. on the dot
        Israeli warplanes with Sidewinders took off
        and scramble-egged the brains of one
        top Lebanese official and blew up
        his motorcade into a powdered sausage

the world is too small and the boundary
too large for these two species of animal
their incestuous love for their neighbor
had not gone unnoticed throughout the human
history—the one that they say repeats itself

        one of them had to be nailed on the cross
        fire around circa one for the lack of love
        another wrote love poems in Arabic pentameter

    that still gallops under the heat of desert
    through mouths of these worshipers of Heaven

no animal species retains such a good memory
for such a long time, a memory that must be
anatomically accurate: tooth for tooth and
eyeball for eyeball, this die-hard ritual
all for the love—of a palm of land

    this dirty hand that must harvest raisins
    with crimson sweetness among the wine-smeared
    rocks of temples where the thick spirit of
    Hammurabi still stands tall residing over the
    conflict among his neighbor-loving subjects

as his ancient brother Solomon generations ahead
as his recent brother Truman generations after
have done diving the baby by the halves, this
difficult chore of slicing flesh from the bone

HAIKU

Fresh summer shower on the green
Mushrooms pop up their round heads
Golf balls scattered on the tee

Highway patrol in the median!
A cobra sunning on the grass
A bite on the Achilles' heel

AT A LOCAL WATERMELON SALE

A nest of them green dinosaur eggs
on the neighbor's green grass, camou-
flaged to the teeth, as if to roll away
alive, forty-two pounds each, blood-
red meat inside with tiny fetus-eyes.

A STOP AT THE BLACK HILLS

Summer
in the Dakota Territory

Red Clouds hoof
a Crazy Horse
at sunset

And a thin strip
of green grass
skirts

these
Black Hills
. . . .

Inside the Wounded
Knee the wind

collects
its breath

Buffalo Black Rocks
under the Wounded Knee

breathe
like Bulls

fallen
in the heat

of one afternoon
on a single

bullet

strayed
at heart

II

At the foothills of the Lying Bull
gathers a large cloud
of dung beetles
In shining armor
metallic black jackets
in a mailed enchainment

Confederate flags flutter
the dust and swastikas red herald
sinuous biceps

Dark knights in full gear ride on
the iron horseback that purrs
its mane in disgust

The air becomes pregnant
this arrogance of self-importance
this everlasting July the Fourth

Black warriors invade the rear
of now a friendly territory
without a boundary

After the midnight of strangeness
in the outback among the bold
mountains of brotherhood

In the Wounded Knee
bare mountains now bear
funny bunny smiles

That spit tattoos on your foreskin
and beer bottles fly like arrows
in memory of the one general

George Armstrong Custer
a name now familiar like
mustard in hot dogs

III

Foreign tourism thrives here
like a thievery under
the broad daylight

White store owners
selling Indian histories
in neat plastic packages
Souvenir hunters now in search of
precious Indian artifacts all
manufactured by Chinese factory

Facts as far away as the setting sun
as rare as a full-blood native
this business of pro-fitting

The Sioux Nation now gone
for a suit and tie
in the federal court

To dance to the tune
of the White heritage
in a legal outrage

The war is far over now
in this day and age
at the root

Of the mountain
that bleeds veins of gold
that will never be undersold

Surrounded by the encroachment
the settlers inch in
day in day out

For the final kill the soft fanfare
of the common man one master
of divination

The Black Hills are now
silent like stone and the legend
is dead cold

In the memory of the living
only a handful wet crows
wing like eagles

Their claws tear the air
that whistles through
the fallen bottles

Twilight now descends
upon the vast of the plain
and at dusk the dust kicks off

A buffalo dance
in thick dark shadows
in ghost-like trance

The hoofs thunder through the memory
your memory and my memory
in the silence that swarms

Their roar beats against the air
like the eagle's feather
the symbol the vision

That flutters its wing at the tip
of the ceremonial pole:
it too wants to fly now

RIVER COLORADO

Yellow fever runs deep
through this vein
of river

A golden rush that snakes
around this vain city
Las Vegas

Carving the Grand Canyon
a large emptiness in
the hollow pan

NOCTURNE

Night is a gigantic cave,
a gaping wound, at the edge
of the cliff, above the seashore.

In the deep throat of the cave dwells
a gargantuan tarantula, a resident spirit,
a Dracula with reddened teeth.

Black-haired and long-thin-legged,
the spider thumbs through the dead
skulls inside the black stomach,

A graveyard where remnants of sunset
linger along the shadows that hide
and seek on tiptoe.

At dusk the mother spider lets out
countless little brown spiders,
and they crawl out one by one.

From their mother's lair,
millions of unhatched eggs spawn
and swarm along the cliff.

And now the night vegetates
within its pit,
the gut.

On its invisible hind leg,
the animal drags them eggs.
All night it hangs the web of life,

In midair, a pitch-black tent, as time
tiptoes through the skulls, like
a gesture wading the wet black jade.

By morning the animal is dead tired.
Digging them eggs from the grave
is a chore of a slave.

At sunrise the spider crawls slowly out,
out from its lair, and dumps over the cliff
myriad of unhatched eggs. They fall like snow.

Among the grains of sands below the shore,
it then scurries back to its grotto tip-
toeing through a few hatched eggs.

Thumbing through the web of light on the wall,
it staggers by the shadow of its own size.
Alarmed, it now starts to eat its own spawn.

MEDITATION

A patch of fog hangs low on treetops
in the wintry wood at my backyard.

A draft of cloud, lost and adrift,
in the stillness of a thin cloth

hanging loose through the jagged
rakes of finger-bone branches.

This pocket of perfection.

On this December morning
there is no wind to speak of.

Then suddenly appear three deer,
a mother and two fawns.

Under the oak standing naked in thought
they munch on stone-frozen nuts.

At this predawn hour in the wood
their jaws crack nuts, like thunder.

AT THE HEART OF SAHARA

—*Adapted from* Saint Exupery

Yesterday I walked without hope....

Today even "hope" has lost its meaning.
Today I walk for the sake of walking.
Like an ox in labor.

Last night I dreamed of paradise.
Full of oranges. Today no oranges exist
to believe in.

In the simmer of desert sands.
I have fallen a number of times.
Among these tall tombs of dunes.

But I don't feel, am no longer
capable of feeling the anguish.

When people discover me—my lips cracked and my eyes
burned—they will probably feel pity on me
that I have suffered a great deal.

But the anguish, the pain, and the sweet refreshing
water of suffering—all these belong to the rich. And
I do no longer own these riches.

On the first night of love-making
young maidens experience the pain
and they cry.

Pain is a sign of life.
And I no longer have the pain.

I have become the desert.

GHOST PAIN (FROM AN AMPUTATED MEMBRANE)

A SAM launched in the heat of 'Nam
I lost my right arm by a napalm

Swear it was a sheer accident and
our guys did not mean no harm

Forty years ago now when the teeth
of TNT bit my right membrane off

—was dangling by a single tendon
all shredded and tattered by the granite rake

But I swear I still wear it there
after all these years

I swear I can still feel my right arm
and each and every one of those fingers

Groping foreign objectives that
I've been searching for all along

Whenever it grabs a head
it won't let go

The blood thickens its grip
right around the neck

And I feel an acute sting
lightening my shoulder down

It refuses to bury the hatchet
though it does not mean no harm now

This perennial ghost will
not surrender its soul

A memory where ghosts still linger
eating away a part of recall

DEAD BROOK

Hidden under the massive sinew of oak branches
that canopy streams of bursting sunbeams below,
and under the outgrowth of thickets lurks a large
open mouth, a shadow of emptiness of one giant
serpent, now defunct and gang dry, in July jungle.

A cavernous dugout veins through the vacant bed-
alimentary-canal that will swallow in one gulp a
squadron of mercenaries alive. Lying there dead still,
among poison ivies and poison oaks, right next to
Darrell's tennis court, is the ghost of the dead dragon.

When I went down there to retrieve miss-rocketed
tennis balls, my heart felt the spirit of the giant snake
brooding among the deposits of large gravel, a dozen
of unhatched dragon eggs now mostly in faded white.

I could smell the sudden chill of being swallowed by
the unexpected charge of this invisible animal, the flood-
water that had carved such a large rage of emptiness
against one Achilles like a mad bull. It was still breath-
ing the hiss of its last locomotion: the open mouth
could have swallowed large boulders alive in a squint.

For a moment, caught aghast inside the belly of the
open tomb, I could hear the deafened roar of the raging
beast that had once terrorized the red-dirt, racing on
down and down onto this large man whose heart was
caught between his teeth, a snow-white jelly bean.

SPRING AT BOSNIA

Today Bosnians and Croats renewed
their war efforts. Some proved
their mettle; others, their metal.

The dead were quickly dispatched into
the shallow graves in the backyard.
Meat-packs in see-through plastics.

Then they set houses ablaze. Some burnt
to the ground. Others, half-burnt,
stood mute, in fuming smolder.

In the spitting distance, a solo machine
gun gave away a staccato applause into
the air, thick smoke now in retreat.

Frightened and at large, flocks of
cattle and sheep roamed empty streets,
as if to take a walkabout.

They wandered into the narrow dirt road
of the hamlet, now devoid of voices.
Except the whispers of the smoke.

Long before the soldiers came, spring had
seized the village. But the trees bore
empty winds, the grass still hoary.

Only apricots and peaches were in full blossom,
a quiet explosion along the torn fences.
They looked eerie, beautiful, and odd:

In the air, their charred fingers of winter
held high flames, bony rakes with
ethereal flowers at the tip.

Among the ruins was an old woman, moving
around the rubble with a garden hose,
water trickling down from its mouth.

She wore a mask of a catatonic as she
put out the fire that still cindered,
hidden, among the ashes.

EMPTY

One leaf, after another, and another.

The sharp wind harps a twang, breaking
the neck bone.

The fall is within us. Once again
in this realm of shadows.

The inaudible dirge plectrums at the
throat of all living dead.

In Hades shadows come and go, sifting
through fingers like impalpable mist.

Wavering like a dream.
These gestures of being.

UNDER THE AUTUMNAL SILVER MOON

the evening breeze
nibbles delicately
in and out through
the open window

outside
the waned beams
of shadow
play hide-and-seek
among the darkened trees

in the bedroom
long skirts of curtains
swell by the lick
of stiff breeze
the milky satin canvas
intermittently
waves deep and brief

quietly
standing on her tiptoe
on my bed balancing in the light
of dancing shadows
Diana peels her pale pear-skin
sheds diaphanous nighties
of silken flowers
one leaflet
after another
ripples down

she thins petals
of paper-white pear flowers and
the leaves fall surreptitiously smooth
on her firm ankles

steel cool and smooth
making a pile of slow-
bursting silky
cascade

in the dark
sitting on the bed
I watch breathlessly
how her shedding skin
makes ripples around
the white beams
dancing in and out through
the shadow
till my lips touch her
bare breast

A TORRENTIAL RAIN

A supercell devours the sun.

A dim dime asphyxiated in the gut,
gobbled up by the evil smoke, closing in
fast at the throat of heaven.

A monstrous black catfish in the sky,
drooping-heavy, pregnant with
burdens, of millions,
of unhatched eggs.

Then cell-burst, tearing the gut
open. A soaking onrush of eggs,
pelting on the tin-top of cars,

stranded fish, on land,
swimming in the puddles
of mud.

A KID-PREACH IN THE PLAYGROUND

I don't know whose dog it is.
It's been stranded and strayed into our school yard
of late. This yellow yelping dog. Without a leash.

This puny pup, with dried streaks of snot-green
that sideburns, hounds our school district every day.
Whining the New Testament in doggerel.

"Shit, Fahrrr, Damnayshun!" it snarls its canine.
All three of them it has. What scares me the most
are the widening gaps between them. You can see its

bubbly venom spitting right through your face.

With the sullen, reddened pouch bulging,
it will aim right at your face and gnarl hell a yell,
a Hectoring belly bark. Suddenly, you are doomed,
accursed, and accused. "You, goddamned sinner."

I often wonder if this little teach is really through
with his paperwork, the toilet training. Because I
often catch him dead pissing at the pole on campus.

His urine is medicinal. It gathers a cloud of passers-by.
I often wonder what fear, what nightmare, what daredevils
loom in its little brain, composed of mere three cells?

I often wonder, too, who could be its owner? Who
could be this desperate to drive their young out onto
the street? Demanding it sell its unfurred skin to strangers.

Have you seen this dog lately? If you have, please
call the animal control.

CONDORS

A messenger of blacken death
lungs the Andean death valley,
its steel wing tips raking the air.

A shadow of satanic harbinger
hovers to knife through the blue,
blocking the arrows of the sun

from the eyes of the living, bring-
ing in the mist of cloud forever,
rolling mountains floating in clouds.

Its iron talons tear and tatter the
Andean pencilings, jagged bluffs,
ragging in a manner of no matter.

The wailing high wind howls long,
pipes the death of a soul, depart-
ing, beyond the shroud of clouds.

Like the Peruvian flute that wind-
pipes in natural candor, celebrating
the coming of the blacken embrace.

AN ARTIST

There, over the vertical bluff, stands the old pine.
It lungs the sea air, adrift, over the wailing waves.

He almost stands erect against the sharp elements
that bite through the bone of being. When accidental

axes cut deep into his flesh he bleeds in silence he
tears the transparent gum he swallows the black
agony, raw. Alone.

This is his only defense, a natural reaction, the inertia
of the root, the center groping for a few drops of
dry H_2O among the rocks. To go on is insane.

To survive the pine, the tree crawls, climbs cliffs,
dust by dust, dew by dew, inches at a time.

Now and then, from the bumpy bark, keen observers unearth his blood-coagulation, the burning anguish, the icy tears in the wild—the yellowing amber of an old wound.

He refused to let go. There, a tiny bug millennia old
congeals its dream to become one day a butterfly.

A wing to fly away *free* from itself.

HERE LIES THE LAST BREED THE CHEETAH

This spectacular speck of long-legged,
speckled ghost *Acinonyx jubatus* can
split atoms of air between his teeth,
between his non-retractable claws.

With a stealthy grace of a feline, it
sweeps up the wild wind, catches it,
in midair, by the neck, in electric sprint,
a perfect species fit for the Olympics.

Faster than any in the living memory of this
planet, the phantom leaves nothing behind
except the gossamer-thin cloth of dust
that collapses, twisting its slender neck,

Upon its own weight—the telltale nightgown
of an enchantress among the bushes.
Another wild game, another victim,
another survival.

The black-spotted shadow haunts the minds,
those soft-eyed gazelles, their salad in abundance,
ubiquitous as grass—their pronking resistance,
a mere bluff of a brown flea.

Yet this supreme machine that skins a gazelle
for a lampshade has its days marked and numbered:
they have been isolated in nature far too long,
on a small island of gene pool of interbreeding.

Incestuously calling themselves brothers and sisters,
and cousins and nephews in vein. Only one out of
three survives the battle of existence in captive,
adrift on an island in the sea of evolution.

Someday gazelles will have to visit the museum
to pay their homage to their ruler, so graceful, sleek,
and enchanting, to marvel at their feline grace, this speck
of ghost, the perfect breed in the imperfect world.

This bringer of black silence.

CAR AIR CONDITIONER

During the heat of July the gooseflesh
Jack Frost hides its tail under the deep freeze
freon inside the iron icebox under the hood.

Inside its lead coffin, playing dead dormant,
the cold-blooded bastard breathes coolant,
the freezing concoction of liquid air.

Now merely sustaining its quiver out of sight,
the foolhardy old man aches from summer,
a migraine fever worse than a winter storm.

Decrepit and defunct as dry ice, he cannot
even lift his finger, caught dead among steel
jaws of engine block that holds its neck tight.

There, he is as honest as dead in July heat,
playing possum, the slimy cold creep, as
docile as domestic doggone in the teeth.

As he hibernates he breathes liquid nitrogen,
the hoary frost rime, through his plastic nostrils,
the only breathing hole that sustains the old glory.

Once in a while inside the coffin of our cars
we remember the old man and his rage;
for now, we are grateful for his dying breath.

THE DEALER

In his garden he grows nothing
out of this world. But a few

garden-variety of headstones,
these faceless faces, smooth
tabula rasa immaculata.

There, in mute stony silence, headless
trunks await their Judgment Day,
—in capital.

This is the Stumbo Street. (No,
not an abbreviation for Stupid Dumbo.)
This is just a retreat where I live.

In his garden grows nothing extra-
ordinary. But rows of fresh-cut
tombstones, like roses.

He has lined 'em up, perfectly,
them their torsos.

Stumps of body parts thus bake,
in neat rows of three, their
marble-skin, buck-naked.

These unblinking blank faces, they are
yours and mine, would not even
stare at you in broad daylight.

Standing there shoulder to shoulder,
they are frozen, immobile, like soldiers.

In his front yard, even the blood-rusted
street sign plays a practical joke:

Leaning sideways, it impersonates
a shadow of a cross.

LOOKING AT THE MAP OF AFRICA IN BLACK, WHITE, AND GRAY

Look at this skull.

This broken piece of pottery. A fractured,
blackened granite. With sockets wide as
the Nile and empty like the Lake Victoria.

A missing molar is Madagascar. Over there.

Fallen off from the toothache. Of fossilizing.
No other body parts endured the tyranny.
Of time—the open mouth.

National borders are cracks. In the skull.
A jigsaw puzzle of jagged bits of bones. Countries
are anatomical chips—glued over. Be careful.

Mali, Niger, Chad, Sudan, Kenya, Zaire,
Angola, Malawi, Namibia, and Zambia.

The territorial struggle for the missing link,
the Sphinx that mastered the art of erection.
In the thick of the Dark Continent—ex nihilo.

The fractured patchwork of human hull
now stands dry and dull. A knotty point sticks out,
halfway through, knifing the layers of sediments.

After many a monsoon, the exhumed skull breathes,
finally, out of grave, of deposits, of frozen time.
Its flesh eaten away by the grains of elements.

Look at this fractured skull. Surfaced lately.
Between the Atlantic and the Indian Oceans.
Whether you like it or not, the eyesore sticks out.

A POET

There lives a bristlecone con pine,
upon a desert, out of nowhere.

An old nut, full of knotty sores,
he is an asymmetrical screw.

Twisted by wrenching turns, warped,
buckled, and rickety with gnarls.

Bowlegged and knock-kneed and
pigeon-toed, the dwarf hangs on.

A natural bonsai in a drying tea pot,
he tries hard to grow. Inward.

An inch in a hundred years, a ring
at a time, in everlasting drought.

All unto himself, he is a miniature
universe. An ever-grin, tooth and nail.

There goes the nut. Mostly talking
to himself, on the edge of insanity.

Grown accustomed to blasting sands,
scorching winds, and wintry droughts.

He'd shut down everything else to
nurture his soul on a single strand of life.

Hidden deep inside the thicken bark,
mutilated, askew, like a contortionist.

There he congeals a drop of water,
molecule by molecule, like a

hunchbacked monk, counting
millennia, crumb by crumb.

A BLIND DATE

It happened in the heart of a winter.
Frozen, I had but one date that year.
Pressing forties, I knew then, my luck
has run out: I had become a born loser.

One day in February, a mutual friend,
known as a witch matchmaker, gave
me a phone number of this girl. I don't
know. Said the wench was tall, in her
thirties, long brown hair, green eyes,
with them big, bovine Oklahoma joints.

What the hell. Ain't got nothing to lose,
nothing going: beggars mustn't choose.
So I called her up and out. A native of
Shawnee, OK, she wasn't familiar with
Stillwater, OK, except for the Walmart,
the Stillwater Cultural Center. Oh, well.

As I stood there in front of the Wal, in my
dating uniform, I felt funny like a Salvation
Army private minus bell. Many women of
her description milled in around 6:00 p.m.

Watching the herd of independent minds
I prayed fast to Lord, in silence: "I know I
done sin, but not this one or that, oh, please."
Then came the lady in her shining pickup.
First I didn't know she was waving at me.

At the Stillwater Oyster Bay, she ordered
a lobster, repeat a lobster, a high-dollar de-
luxe at the joint, while I sucked on a piece
of dry chicken leg. You are right.

To camouflage my shock, I had to bullshit about
anything, my head smoking while tabbing
that this woman, this lady, ordered a lobster
and a bottle of wine on our first blind date!

While protesting against the gun-ownership,
my head was fuming, 'cause I knew I just had
to get my damn money's worth: a year later,
I married this girl with big bovine OK joints.

AT THE CENTER

After the daily morning meditation
I grab my bamboo poles and head for
a Walden Pond in the middle of Oklahoma
nowhere.

In the open prairie, the sky grows limitless.
Wide, far, and blue.

Black Angus cows have already gone to take
shelter under wild oaks and pecans in the
far-away woods. Hoppers pop as I walk.

The flaming July gust blows long heatwaves,
bends tall Johnsongrass low on the hedges.

In the middle of the pasture, the pond boils
with ripples, drying up molecule by molecule.

I cast my luck far into the brown silt where
the perch have hatched this year's newlings.

Nothing bites except for a school of gnats,
caught accidentally in the gust of red wind.

In midday, the sun stings. I scarf my neck,
tilt my hat, and stand firm on the bank.

The sun behind my back, sometimes I catch
myself within my own shadow. Perfect.

THE SORROW OF THOREAU

There was a bug in the tableland of
Massachusetts, a flat elevated region
near a glass of water, napkins of fields,
toothpick chopsticks woods at Concord.

Decades ago, it was deposited there, as
an egg, in the alburnum of the green and
living tree, insulated within the home-
spun silk of its own cocoon. The tree

then was metamorphosed into an old
table of apple-tree wood, which had
withstood in a New England farmer's
kitchen for nearly sixty years, frozen.

For all its Harvard varnish, the hardwood
was never gainfully employed, never truly
loved by another flesh, leaving no choice
but to walk through local yard sales until

it ended up in the kitchen of an immigrant
Concord farmer. By the heat of an earthen-
ware, the germ one day woke up, and the
worm started to glow and grub and gnaw

the layers of cellulose. Thoroughly, its
larva of thought ate the concentric layers
of woodenness in the dead dry life of society.
For years, it gutted every available page

of Homer, the Bible, Virgil, Ovid, Plutarch,
Brahmins, Buddha, Mencius, Confucius till
one day the farmer heard its nibbling in the
absolute quietude of his dinner and dessert.

The astonished family of man sat around
the festive board and witnessed the beautiful
winged creature crawl out to enjoy a perfect
summer—waking up the world in its quiver.

IMPLOSION

Tall stood the Federal Building
of the United States of America.

Shaken in the terror of shell-shock,
it just stood there catatonic like a

young soldier who lost his Stars
and Stripes, his wits gone in war.

Legs blown off, his tendons hung
loose-rebars, his blood spattered

in eight directions, a machine gun
spray. On his torn legs, he stood

refusing to go down, refusing to
knee the dirt, his pants tattered

like a rag shredded by the iron rake
of shrapnel, the teeth of the timid.

The wind cut deep into his wound,
exposing disemboweled intestines.

Eyes frozen, he stood there mute,
dazed, rain or shine, for long months,

fighting against himself and his wits,
refusing to go down, refusing to

bite the dust. In the end, they had to
collapse his lungs from within, chok-

ing his windpipe inward. He stag-
gered and plopped down with a

whimper, sending off black fumes of anger that ran like tumbleweeds.

The Federal Building of the United States of America was no more.

COGITO, ERGO SUM

The sum of our existence
is a bag of reasoning, a
sag we drag to our tomb.

No matter where we go,
we brag our little cargo,
full of incidental garbage.

From womb we carry this
burden of evidence, a proof
of disproof. We lock up

our souls in the gaol cell,
this frigid cold abstract
we call a free, open mind.
Sadists to the bone, we
lick our back with whips.

Blood-hounding our body
and mind with acute thinking
of unthinking, we murder
our mind in entertainment.

Like a herd of cattle, we fear
this reflection of ourselves,
this shadow that dogs us
from day one till last.

Day and night this invisible
black snake lashes our gaunt
souls, this empty house, where
a loud wind walks through.

Just look around and listen to
this religious mongering, a
shadow talking to another, a
fear taking another in arms.

Reasoning is God's curse,
the worst of all gifts. It whips
us worse than cattle. Ergo,
ergo, cogito ergo doom.

JULY FULL MOON

The world is a giant cave,
a sublunary tunnel, lit dim
by a colossal candle.

An enlarged soiled silver
platter reflecting upon its
own face of opaqueness.

Shadows flicker dark flames
in the wind of imagination,
a black silk that veils

this underworld, a view
through a worn-out
cheesecloth.

Under the immense shadow
insects war tearing up each
other, eating up the edges

of the cheese. Night broadens
under the fake sun like
dust of dusk under

a moth's wing.

DAO OF LAO-TSE

mountain is mountain
river is river
sky, sky

mountain rivers
river skies
sky mountains

river mountains
sky rivers
mountain skies

mountain river sky
dirt water air
birth process death

the I is eye
burning fire
watching the flow

eye I am
out of here
present

Born in South Korea, Yoon Sik Kim had served as an officer in the Republic of Korea Air Force for five years before he came to America. He earned his Master's from the University of Oklahoma and his Ph. D. from Oklahoma State University, specializing in Ezra Pound and Modern Poetry. Having taught for more than 30 years at the college level, he now teaches part-time while sharpening the blade of his wordsmithing. Married to an Okie, he homesteads in the outback of Oklahoma, where he lives with his wife, children, horses, and honeybees on a farm.

The New York Quarterly Foundation, Inc.
New York, New York

Poetry Magazine

Since 1969

Edgy, fresh, groundbreaking, eclectic—voices from all walks of life.

Definitely NOT your mama's poetry magazine!

The *New York Quarterly* has been defining the term contemporary American poetry since its first craft interview with W. H. Auden.

Interviews • Essays • and of course, lots of poems.

www.nyquarterly.org

No contest! That's correct, NYQ Books are NO CONTEST to other small presses because we do not support ourselves through contests. Our books are carefully selected by invitation only, so you know that NYQ Books are produced with the same editorial integrity as the magazine that has brought you the most eclectic contemporary American poetry since 1969.

Books

nyqbooks.org

poetry at the edge™

www.ingramcontent.com/pod-product-compliance
Lightning Source LLC
LaVergne TN
LVHW011427080426
835512LV00005B/305